Railways & Recollections 19

Contents

© Chris Harris 2014
Photographs by Ray Ruffell © The NOSTALGIA *Collection* archive, unless otherwise credited

First published in 2014

British Library Cataloguing in Publication Data

A catalogue record for this book is available from the British Library.

ISBN 978 1 85794 428 0

Silver Link Publishing Ltd
The Trundle
Ringstead Road
Great Addington
Kettering
Northants NN14 4BW

Tel/Fax: 01536 330588
email: sales@nostalgiacollection.com
Website: www.nostalgiacollection.com

Printed and bound in the Czech Republic

Frontispiece: **BURY INTERCHANGE** This station was opened on Monday 17 March 1980, replacing Bury Bolton Street and providing a bus/rail interchange close to Bury town centre. This route from Manchester to Bury had been electrified by the Lancashire & Yorkshire Railway using a unique 1,200V third-rail side-contact system, and the pre-Grouping stock survived until 1959 when it was replaced by two-car electric multiple units built at British Railways Wolverton Works especially for the line – as exemplified by this train about to return to Manchester at 1644 on Saturday 5 July. The recently opened station seen here was to have a life of just over 11 years, as the route from Bury Interchange to Manchester via Besses o' th' Barn was closed from 17 August 1991 for conversion to tramway operation as part of the Manchester Metrolink system.

Introduction: Starting a new decade

In many ways 1980 was an interesting and rather turbulent year that led to one of the more unsettled periods in the recent history of the UK. The year was only a couple of days old when the steel industry was hit by its first strike since 1926.

The economy went into recession during June, unemployment was rising towards 2 million (it would peak at 3.2 million in the mid-1980s), while inflation stood at 18%. In a generally unpopular budget taxes were raised while Government expenditure was cut; the announcement that benefits paid to the families of strikers would be cut by £12 per week met with a particular outcry. Many economists urged that a different course should be taken, but to no avail.

A riot in the St Paul's district in Bristol on 2 April, which resulted in 19 people being injured, was a grim foretaste of the social unrest that was brewing in the country and which would erupt more violently elsewhere the following year. In May a siege at the Iranian embassy in London was ended when SAS troops stormed the building, releasing 26 hostages and killing five terrorists.

The Olympic Games in Moscow were boycotted by a number of countries, including Canada and the USA, in protest at the Soviet intervention in Afghanistan; nonetheless 80 countries took part and Britain's athletes came home with 21 medals (five gold, seven silver and nine bronze).

Ronald Reagan defeated Jimmy Carter to become President of the USA in November. And there was very sad news from the USA the following month when John Lennon was shot dead in New York.

On a more cheerful note, two of the new gadgets of 1980 were Rubik's cube and the Sony Walkman, while development of the theme park began at Alton Towers. New cars introduced during the year included the BL Metro, the Morris Ital and the Mark 3 Ford Escort. Long-distance express coach services were deregulated in October, and this led to increased competition with trains on some routes for a time.

On the railways there were some encouraging developments in 1980. April saw the reopening to the public of the Glasgow subway system after a three-year closure during which the line, previously almost a living museum with carriages dating back to the 1890s, was completely modernised. On 11 August the first section of the Tyne & Wear Metro (from Haymarket to Tynemouth) opened and ushered in a new era for urban transport in Britain. By the summer of 1980 InterCity 125 HSTs were in use on the routes from Paddington to Bristol, South Wales and the West of England, and also on the East Coast Main Line. Until the onset of the recession things had looked set fair for InterCity, but later in the year costs were rising while revenue, especially from business travel, was reduced; action to trim costs resulted in some service reductions towards the end of 1980.

There were considerable efforts to stimulate optional travel by rail, including free ticket promotions with such diverse partners as Kelloggs and Lever Brothers. To mark the 150th anniversary of the Liverpool & Manchester Railway, British Rail arranged a re-enactment of the Rainhill Trials followed by a cavalcade of steam, diesel and electric locomotives and stock illustrating the development of railways over 150 years. This enjoyable and well-organised celebration took place on 24, 25 and 26 May.

A shock that rail managers (and passengers) in Wales could have done without was the discovery of serious damage to Barmouth Bridge on the Cambrian Coast Line caused by worms boring through more than 70 of the timber piles supporting the structure. The bridge had to be closed to all traffic until repairs were carried out, and there were fears that this scenic (and socially valuable) line might be closed altogether, but fortunately funds were found to repair the bridge, which reopened in May 1981.

Let us look back to a year when the average annual wage was £6,000, a pint of beer cost 35p, a loaf of bread was 33p and petrol cost 28p per litre. Let us revisit 1980…

Chris Harris
Poole, Dorset

Cornish Rhapsody

PENZANCE We begin our look back at 1980 in the west of Cornwall. The first station on this site at Penzance was opened in 1852 by the West Cornwall Railway and was a wooden structure; the granite-walled buildings and overall roof seen here were provided by the Great Western Railway, which rebuilt the station in 1879 and made further improvements in 1937-38. These photographs were taken on Thursday 30 October 1980. The first illustrates the intending traveller's initial view of the trains when accessing the station from the street-level entrance through the Travel Centre, with stairs leading down to the platforms.

The second view is looking back along the platforms towards the main buildings, with the stairs to the Travel Centre and street-level exit just visible top right behind the InterCity 125 HST unit. Notice also the lower-level exit from Platform 3 on the left; this is given more prominent signage for passengers leaving the station, and was to become the main entrance and exit when the premises were refurbished in the early 1980s.

PENZANCE A favourite place to watch trains at Penzance has always been looking over the wall from Chyandour Cliff. The weather was very dull and misty when Ray Ruffell took this photograph on the morning of Sunday 26 October, but there is plenty of railway interest to be seen. Some shunting of hauled stock is taking place in Platform 1 nearest to the camera, while InterCity 125 HST units Nos 253028 and 253005 await custom at Platforms 2 and 3 respectively. Platform 4, in the open on the far side of the station, is occupied by a van train headed by Class 50 locomotive No 50044. Entering service on the London Midland Region as No D444, this locomotive was transferred to the Western Region following the completion of the electrification between Crewe and Glasgow in 1974 and given the name *Exeter*. It was withdrawn in January 1991, and has subsequently been preserved by the Class 50 Alliance. Note the Class 47 and Class 50 locomotives visible in the sidings beyond Platform 4.

1980 Happenings (1)

January
- Nationwide strike by workers at British Steel begins.

February
- Government announces cuts in state benefits paid to strikers.
- More than 11,000 job losses in Wales predicted by British Steel.
- Robin Cousins wins gold for figure skating at the Winter Olympics held at Lake Placid, USA.

March
- A newspaper survey suggests that 60% of Britons are dissatisfied with Margaret Thatcher's Conservative Government, which is now trailing behind Labour in opinion polls.
- Robert Runcie is enthroned as Archbishop of Canterbury.
- Alexander Kielland accommodation platform in North Sea collapses when massive wave hits one of its supporting legs, resulting in death of 123 oil-rig workers.

April
- Strike by British Steel workers ends.
- UK reaches agreement with Spain to reopen border with Gibraltar.
- Zimbabwe becomes independent of UK.

May
- Siege at Iranian Embassy in London ends when SAS storms building, freeing 26 hostages and killing five of the six terrorists involved.
- British Aerospace is privatised.
- Public outcry after inquest rules that teacher Blair Peach, killed during demonstration in 1979, died as result of misadventure.

June
- British Leyland announces Morris Ital range of cars.
- Police marksman accidentally shoots pregnant 16-year-old Gail Kinchen in Birmingham, killing her and her unborn child.
- Government announces that US nuclear cruise missiles will be located at Greenham Common in Berkshire and Molesworth in Cambridgeshire.
- The 'tanner' (pre-decimal sixpence) is withdrawn from circulation.

ST MICHAEL'S MOUNT This picturesque island lies just off the Cornish coast at Marazion. At low tide it can be reached on foot by a causeway from the mainland, while at other times access has to be by boat. The Mount has been the home of the St Aubyn family, who occupy the Castle, for centuries, and some other families in the small community have also lived there for generations. The Castle, together with a church, sits at the top of the Mount and is reached from the shore by steep pathways. During the early years of the 20th century a narrow-gauge cable-hauled tramway was built to convey goods up to the Castle. Opened in 1912, the line runs almost entirely in tunnel and has a maximum gradient slightly steeper than 1 in 2. From the lower station near the quay the line runs in a tunnel beneath the gardens, then upwards through the rock of the Mount to reach the upper station at the Castle. Still operational 100 years after opening, the tramway is used to carry goods up to the Castle – passengers are not carried. These photographs were taken near the lower station on Sunday 26 October 1980 and show the narrow-gauge track disappearing into the tunnel prior to the steep climb up to the Castle.

NEWQUAY Since the closure of the line from Chacewater and Perranporth in February 1963, all passenger trains to Newquay have left the main line at Par and run via St Blazey, Luxulyan and Roche. The 1140 service from Par, a two-car diesel multiple unit (DMU) 'power twin', had just terminated at Platform 1 when photographed by Ray Ruffell on Tuesday 28 October 1980. The station was still reasonably intact at that time, although the canopy over Platforms 2 and 3 had been cut back in 1964. Subsequently the tracks serving Platforms 1 and 3 have been abolished, all trains now arriving at and departing from the former Platform 2. This has been resurfaced, while 'rationalisation' of the premises has resulted in the demolition of the attractive buildings and canopies illustrated in the photographs, although a stylish wave-shaped canopy has recently been provided over the concourse area behind the buffer stop. In the 21st century, through trains from London, the Midlands and the North still come down the branch to Newquay during the holiday season, reflecting the continued popularity of the resort, not least as the principal centre for surfing in the UK.

Right: **PAR** Around an hour or so earlier than the photographs on the previous page, the same two-car DMU awaits connecting passengers from the 0725 service from London Paddington, which is just running into Platform 1 on the right. Passenger usage figures have grown at this station in recent years, although not many people can be seen on the rather inclement morning when this photograph was taken. Note the old Great Western Railway bench in the foreground.

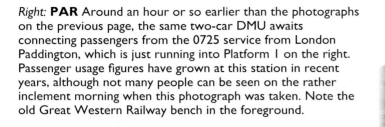

Left: **SALTASH** The HST forming the 1010 Penzance to London Paddington service passes out of Cornwall into Devon as it crosses the Royal Albert Bridge over the River Tamar on Thursday 30 October. Designed by Isambard Kingdom Brunel, this elegant two-span bowstring suspension bridge is a masterpiece of 19th-century engineering and was officially opened by His Royal Highness Prince Albert on 2 May 1859. It is worth noting that the adjacent road bridge across the River Tamar, part of which is just visible above the front of the train, did not come into use until October 1961.

EXETER BASIN The Branch Line Society's 'South Devon Railtour' ran from Bristol Temple Meads on Saturday 10 May 1980, and visited a number of locations not normally served by passenger trains. One such was the short freight-only branch to Exeter City Basin, at that time used mainly by oil traffic and subsequently closed in 1983. The train stopped on the branch for the passengers to alight and explore before returning to the main line. It then proceeded to Newton Abbot, where the three-car Metropolitan-Cammell DMU set being used for the railtour was declared a failure owing to a broken spring. With commendable promptness a locomotive-hauled train was commandeered to take the railtour participants on to Plymouth.

Catch it while you can: The 'South Devon Railtour'

CATTEWATER On arrival at Plymouth station a replacement DMU was provided for the rest of the railtour, this time a Gloucester RC&W three-car Cross Country set. The freight-only branch to Cattewater had been part of the LSWR and later the Southern Railway system in Plymouth. By 1980 it was in decline; coal traffic had virtually ceased after the closure of Plymouth 'A' power station in 1974, and in due course the closure of Plymouth 'B' power station and the Fison's fertiliser plant in 1981 was to seal the line's fate. Passengers are seen returning to the train after a 5-minute photo-stop.

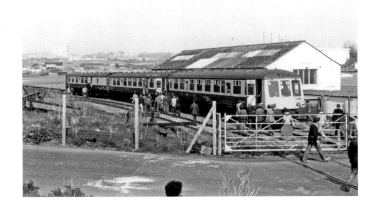

Glasgow's 'Clockwork Orange'

GLASGOW ST ENOCH Opened in December 1896, the Glasgow Underground operates a circular route 6.5 miles long with 15 stations; trains run clockwise around the outer track of the circle and anti-clockwise around the inner track. With an unusual gauge of 4 feet and a tunnel diameter of 11 feet, the trains are particularly small for an urban transport system. Cable haulage was used from the opening of the line until 1935, when the original 1896 carriages were converted to third-rail electric operation at 600 volts. By the mid-1970s the line was very run-down; passenger numbers were falling, the carriages were 80 years old, and there was a general air of dilapidation. In May 1977 the system was temporarily closed to allow major refurbishment to take place, and it reopened to passengers in April 1980 with a bright new image. The new trains were built by Metro-Cammell at Birmingham, and the popularity of the restored service is illustrated by these photographs taken on Saturday 31 May, which show exterior and interior views of the diminutive trains. The livery used was a bright orange, and this, together with the fact that the trains operate on a circular route, soon led to the reopened system becoming (affectionately) known as the 'Clockwork Orange'.

Right: **GLASGOW ST ENOCH** When the system opened in 1896, the surface building here was the headquarters of the Glasgow District Subway Railway Company; a delightful structure complete with turrets and finials and designed by James Miller, it was preserved when the subway was modernised in 1977-80 but is no longer used as a ticket office or travel information centre – it became a branch of Café Nero in 2009. A new entrance to the station had been provided when the line reopened in 1980, and below ground St Enoch station had also been restyled with side platforms replacing the former double-sided island platform. This is clearly illustrated in this photograph, also taken on Saturday 31 May; the relatively small size of the trains is also readily apparent.

Below: **BISHOPTON** British Railways had also introduced some stylish electric trains in the Glasgow

area. Electrification of the North Clyde and Cathcart Circle lines in 1960-61 had seen the provision of a distinctive fleet of multiple units (later Class 303), which were initially painted in Caledonian blue – soon becoming known as the 'Blue Trains'. When the lines from Glasgow Central to Gourock and Wemyss Bay were electrified in 1967 a batch of 19 very similar units (Class 311) was provided for them. The interiors of these units were very comfortable, with deep-sprung 3+2 seating and glass partitions between the saloons and the cabs, giving passengers at the front of the train an excellent forward view along the line – even after the original wrap-round windscreen had been replaced by toughened flat glass as seen here. Unit No 311095 calls at Bishopton while operating the 1245 service from Gourock to Glasgow Central on Friday 30 May. The last of the Class 311 units was withdrawn from passenger service in November 1990; some of the earlier Class 303 sets remained in traffic, but in a refurbished form that had considerably altered their interior appointments.

Channel Islands link

WEYMOUTH By 1980 one of the only remaining locations in England where trains carried passengers along a section of the public highway was at Weymouth, where boat trains connecting with the Sealink ships to and from the Channel Islands used the street tramway along Commercial Road and Custom House Quay between Weymouth Town and Weymouth Quay stations. Although this provided a very convenient rail/sea interchange for passengers, operational problems rather beyond the control of the railway sometimes caused delays. Because the tracks along the roadway were generally not in frequent use for trains, it was quite common for the boat train to find its passage blocked by a badly parked vehicle, despite the efforts of both the local and the British Transport Police. Here a Waterloo-bound Channel Islands Boat Express hauled by a Class 33 diesel-electric locomotive can be seen waiting while an errant vehicle is removed – no doubt this resulted in the writing of a lost-time ticket. The last Channel Islands Boat Express to use the tramway ran on 26 September 1987; Weymouth Quay station, which had been rebuilt in the 1960s, still stands in the 21st century and at the time of writing is used as offices by Condor Ferries. *Brian Jackson*

Inset: **WEYMOUTH** When through boat trains were not running passengers were transferred between Weymouth Town and Weymouth Quay stations by Western National bus. During the 1970s a dedicated Bristol FLF in Sealink livery was provided for this, but there was always the problem of passengers' luggage, which had to follow behind in a railway lorry. In 1980 a Leyland National, fleet number 2823, was painted in Sealink livery and a luggage trailer formerly towed by Routemasters on London Airport services was acquired. Thus newly equipped, 2823 awaits its next duty in Weymouth Town station yard with the former GWR goods shed – now the site of a B&Q store – in the background. *Brian Jackson*

100 years of Royal Blue

EXETER The summer of 1980 saw the celebration of the centenary of Royal Blue coach services; it was in September 1880 that the founder of Royal Blue, Thomas Elliott, was first granted a hackney-carriage licence, and his duties would have included carrying passengers between Holmsley railway station and the Royal Bath Hotel in Bournemouth. From this small beginning the company eventually grew into one of the best-remembered names in express coach services. With the use of motor coaches and an expanding route network after the First World War, Royal Blue was acquired by the Western/Southern National Omnibus Company in 1935 and became part of a pool known as Associated Motorways with a hub at

Cheltenham offering connections to all parts of the country, as well as maintaining services from the West Country to London. Many were sad when the distinctive Royal Blue livery was subsumed into the white of National Express in the early 1970s, and happy memories were revived by this line-up of preserved vehicles *(below)* celebrating the centenary at Exeter coach station. Left to right, they are OTT 98 (new in 1953), OTT 43 (also new in 1953), 617 DDV (1960), HDV 624E (1967) and 253 KTA (1962).

Photographed on the same day, underfloor-engine Bristol LS6G OTT 98 of 1953 *(above right)* can be compared with traditional half-cab Bristol LL6B LTA 898, new in 1951. Note the roof-top luggage racks fitted to both coaches, a feature that Royal

Blue specified for new vehicles until the mid-1950s. Deregulation of express coach services in October 1980 sparked a revival of interest in long-distance coach travel. *Brian Jackson*

Railway paddle steamers in retirement

RIVER THAMES There was a time when a trip on the River Thames guaranteed the sight of a good variety of shipping, but by 1980 this had been much reduced. However, two of the paddle steamers previously employed by the LNER and later British Railways on the Humber ferry were to be seen on the Thames that year.

PS *Wingfield Castle (top)* and sister ship PS *Tattershall Castle* were both built for the LNER by William Gray & Company of Hartlepool in 1934, and both were launched on 24 September that year. Entering service on the ferry route between Hull and New Holland, the ships remained on this duty for many years. In 1973 *Tattershall Castle* was found to be in need of boiler repairs, but these were considered to be not cost-effective, so she was withdrawn from service. *Wingfield Castle* remained for almost another year, bring withdrawn after operating the 1730 crossing from Hull on 14 May 1974. The Humber ferry service was then maintained by DEPV *Farringford* (which had been built in 1948 for the Lymington to Yarmouth service) until the opening of the Humber Bridge on 24 June 1981 eliminated the need for the ferry.

Brought to the Thames after retirement, *Wingfield Castle* was laid up pending decisions on her future. Having proved unsuitable for several projects, eventually she returned to Hartlepool in 1986, where she has been beautifully restored and can be visited at Hartlepool's Maritime Experience. *Tattershall Castle* also came to the River Thames following withdrawal by British Rail, and served as a floating art gallery and conference centre between 1975 and 1981. She was then rebuilt and opened as a public house/entertainment centre, in which role she still remains on the Thames at Victoria Embankment at the time of writing. *Brian Jackson*

BOURNEMOUTH Built by A. & J. Inglis Ltd of Glasgow in 1946 for the LNER as a replacement for an earlier ship of that name that had been lost while taking part in the evacuation of Dunkirk in 1940, PS *Waverley* made her maiden voyage on 16 June 1947 and operated on the River Clyde until withdrawn by Caledonian MacBrayne at the end of the 1973 season. Sold to the Paddle Steamer Preservation Society for £1, PS *Waverley* is now the last sea-going paddle steamer in the world and regularly visits the Bristol Channel, the Thames and the South Coast – where she was photographed alongside Bournemouth Pier in 1980. Disregarding the *Ryde*, which is now in a serious state of decay, only three former railway paddle steamers survive – *Wingfield Castle*, *Tattershall Castle* and *Waverley*. Brian Jackson

SITTINGBOURNE PS *Caledonia* was launched in February 1934 for the Caledonian Steam Packet Company (a subsidiary of the London Midland & Scottish Railway) for operation on the River Clyde. Withdrawn after the 1969 season, she became a floating public house on the River Thames, renamed *Old Caledonia*. Unfortunately damaged beyond repair by a fire in April 1980, her hull was moved to a breaker's yard near Sittingbourne where this photograph of the once proud vessel was taken shortly afterwards. Fortunately her engines were salvaged and are preserved at the Hollycombe Steam Collection, Liphook, Hampshire. *Brian Jackson*

In and around Edinburgh

PRINCES STREET GARDENS Located in the centre of Edinburgh, Princes Street Gardens form the best-known and most visited public park in the city and date from the early 19th century. There was some controversy when the railway linking Haymarket and Edinburgh Waverley was first cut through the Gardens in 1846, and again when the cuttings and tunnels were expanded to take extra tracks between 1892 and 1900. On Wednesday 28 May 1980 a DMU formation is seen passing along the line through the Gardens while forming the 1620 service from Edinburgh Waverley to Dundee. Note some of Edinburgh's landmarks on the skyline: left to right, the Scott Monument, the clock tower of the North British Hotel, and the Scottish National Gallery. When this photograph was taken the North British was part of British Transport Hotels, but it was sold the following year; it still flourishes as a hotel in the 21st century, but has been renamed the Balmoral.

HAYMARKET Opened in 1842, Haymarket was the original head office and terminus of the Edinburgh & Glasgow Railway before the line was extended to Edinburgh Waverley four years later (see above). The fine building, also seen here on Wednesday 28 May, reflects the station's original eminence. Haymarket is well located for the West End of Edinburgh, and in 2011 was the fourth busiest railway station in Scotland in terms of passenger footfall.

MILLERHILL YARD Located just south of Edinburgh, Millerhill Freight Yard was one of the fruits of the 1955 British Railways Modernisation Plan. On Friday 6 June 1980 Class 37 diesel-electric locomotive No 37048 is arriving with a train from the Blue Circle Cement Works at Oxwellmains, near Dunbar. This locomotive was in service for more than 40 years, entering traffic in August 1962 (as No D6748) and being withdrawn in March 2003.

KIRKCALDY A branch line around half a mile long left the Edinburgh-Dundee line at Kirkcaldy to link the rail network with Kirkcaldy Harbour. At the point where the branch diverged the main line was 100 feet above sea level. As a result the harbour branch, as well as turning through 180 degrees during its relatively short length, had a gradient of an incredible 1 in 21. The steepness of the incline, more suited to a theme park than a railway freight branch, is well illustrated in this photograph, taken on Thursday 29 May; the speed restriction of 4mph was a very necessary precaution for trains to be able to stop at the end of the line. The branch to Kirkcaldy Harbour was closed in 1984.

was closed to passengers with the withdrawal of trains from Edinburgh to Glasgow via Bathgate and Airdrie in January 1956, but freight services continued – a touch of irony being that for many years trainloads of new motor cars formed a significant amount of the traffic carried. Passenger services between Edinburgh and Bathgate were restored in 1986 and used a new and rather basic single-platform station built on the site of the 1849 original. In 2007 plans were announced to reinstate passenger services between Edinburgh and Glasgow via Bathgate and Airdrie, and the line was electrified at 25kV AC; services commenced in December 2010. A smart new station was provided at Bathgate, providing excellent accommodation for the passengers using what has already become a popular service.

Above: **PUMPHERSTON OIL SIDINGS**
The extraction of shale oil was once a very significant industry in West Lothian. Experiments in 1946 at the Pumpherston refinery led to the production of synthetic detergents, and while refining of crude oil here ceased in 1962, production of detergents, in later days using imported oil, continued until the plant closed in 1993. Class 25 locomotive No 25231, built at BR Darlington Works in 1963 as No D7581 and in service with British Rail until August 1985, is seen at Pumpherston Oil Sidings on Friday 6 June 1980.

Right: **BATHGATE** The railway reached Bathgate in 1849 and the station seen in this photograph, taken on the same day as the one above, opened as Bathgate (Upper) in 1865. It

Catch it while you can: the 'Xmas Tommy' railtour

PENISTONE Work on the electrification of the route from Manchester to Sheffield and Wath via Woodhead had been started by the LNER in 1938, but was soon put on hold owing to the Second World War. A prototype electric locomotive for the route was completed in 1941 and, after initial testing on the already electrified route between Manchester and Altrincham, was put into storage until the end of hostilities. In 1947, with the advent of electrified services over the Woodhead route clearly still some years away, the prototype was loaned to Netherlands Railways – an action that helped the Dutch with an acute shortage of motive power and also enabled the locomotive to be evaluated under service conditions. The Dutch railwaymen referred to the locomotive as 'Tommy', and this name was applied officially when it returned to British Railways' service in 1952.

By 1980 the Woodhead route across the Pennines was slated for closure, and when the LCGB arranged the 'Xmas Tommy' railtour for 30 December that year it was thought at the time of planning that it would be one of the last trains to use the line, but in the event freight traffic continued until July 1981. Having travelled from Manchester via Woodhead, the railtour pauses for a photo-stop at Penistone; the locomotive is not *Tommy*, but No 76006, built at Gorton Works in 1951 and in service until July 1981.

WORSBOROUGH After visiting Wath, the railtour returned west via the formidable Worsborough Bank, a 3-mile incline with a maximum gradient of 1 in 40, which had required special banking arrangements for coal trains in the days of steam; indeed, banking was still necessary after electrification. For the railtour, sister locomotive No 76054 was provided to assist No 76006 between Wath and Barnsley Junction, and as it heads towards Worsborough Bank the train has attracted a number of observers as daylight fades on this bleak winter afternoon.

Derbyshire delight: Crich Tramway Museum

CRICH A steep walk uphill from Whatstandwell station on the Derby to Matlock branch leads to the National Tramway Museum at Crich. The Tramway Museum Society was formed after the Second World War when it was becoming apparent that in general the outlook for trams in British towns and cities was bleak. This site in a former chalk quarry was acquired in the late 1950s and has been developed into a fascinating 'tramway village' including buildings and period street furniture – such as telephone boxes where you press button A to be connected or button B to get your money back if there is no reply at the other end (remember those?) – in addition to the trams themselves. The museum was well established when Ray Ruffell and his daughter Margaret visited on Wednesday 30 July 1980. Instead of an admission ticket, visitors arriving at Crich receive an old pre-decimal penny when they pay their admission fee; this can then be used to buy a ticket from a tram conductor, which is then valid for unlimited travel on the various trams operating along the demonstration line for the rest of that day.

Two preserved trams from the former Glasgow system are seen here. Car 812 *(below left)* was built in 1900 and was originally a 59-seat open-top car with open platforms at each end. It was rebuilt and renovated several times during its years of service in Glasgow, and by the time of its withdrawal in 1960 had an enclosed top deck and end platforms as seen here. The building to the left of the photograph incorporates the façade of the old Assembly Rooms, Derby; it dates from the 18th century and was relocated to Crich in 1963.

Car 1297, seen on the right of the second photograph, was built for the Glasgow system in 1948 and was therefore only 14 years old when tramway operation ceased in Glasgow in September 1962; this car took part in the final procession around the system prior to closure. The tower on the top of the cliff in the background is Crich Stand, built in 1923 as a memorial to the men of the Sherwood Foresters who were killed during the First World War.

CRICH The rather stylish single-deck tram seen in the first picture was one of a pair built for the Leeds system by local bodybuilders C. H. Roe. The centre entrance/exit vestibule is flanked by two saloons, each with 17 seats, giving a capacity of 34 seated passengers plus up to 32 standing. This tram differed from its visually similar partner by having a very advanced control and braking system. It was No 602 in the Leeds fleet and entered service in June 1953 carrying a special Royal purple and ivory livery to mark its introduction in Coronation year. Trialled across the Leeds system before finding regular use on the Hunslet route, this car was liked for its quiet running and good performance, while passengers appreciated the comfortable seating but were less impressed when the lower number of seats meant that they had to travel standing. In any event, the decision to progressively abandon tramway operation in Leeds was also taken in 1953, and No 602 was withdrawn from service in 1957; the final trams ran in the city on 7 November 1959.

Single-deck car No 674 is unique as the only American tram in the collection at Crich. It was built in 1939 for the 3rd Avenue Transit System in New York, with seating for 48 passengers. This tram was one of more than 40 that were shipped from America to Vienna after the Second World War as part of the Marshall Aid plan; it became No 4225 in the Vienna fleet, where it remained in service until May 1969.

CRICH During the post-war period all of the remaining British tramway undertakings were abandoned with one significant exception – the Promenade route in Blackpool and inter-urban continuation to Fleetwood. Moreover, the Blackpool system has seen huge investment during the 21st century, and new easy-access 'Flexity 2' trams built by Bombardier commenced operation between Starr Gate and Fleetwood from Wednesday 4 April 2012. Blackpool Transport is also operating heritage trams on the line during some weekends and school holidays between Easter and the start of the illuminations in August. And while the Blackpool system is the only remaining 'first generation' tramway in the UK, new examples of rail-based urban transit systems have

emerged in past 20 or so years, such as the Sheffield Supertram and the Nottingham Express Transit System, to name but two.

A reminder of earlier days in the history of Blackpool's trams was sampled by Ray's 11-year-old daughter Margaret, who enjoyed a ride on preserved car No 49 at Crich on Wednesday 30 July 1980; this tram had entered service at Blackpool in 1926.

Crich Tramway Village is normally open daily from April to October inclusive; admission, at the time of writing, includes unlimited vintage tram rides and, with many other nostalgic delights to enjoy, a visit to this unique attraction is highly recommended.

508s on the Southern

Right: **CLAPHAM JUNCTION** Although modern electric suburban stock with power-operated sliding doors and open saloon accommodation had been introduced in Liverpool during the late 1930s, it was not until the early 1970s that the first experimental electric multiple units (EMUs) of this type appeared on the Southern Region. Built at BR Engineering's York Works, there were two units of four cars and one of two cars; after trials during 1972 they entered passenger service in June 1973 and were mostly to be found on services from London Waterloo to Hampton Court, Shepperton or Chessington South. These experimental vehicles

had all been withdrawn from passenger service by December 1976, thereafter spending some time stored at Strawberry Hill and East Wimbledon; an unidentified Class 33 diesel-electric locomotive is seen approaching Clapham Junction while returning some of the experimental stock to the Derby Research Centre on Thursday 26 June 1980. Although at that time less than 10 years old, these carriages were never again used in service, and were ultimately broken up.

Left: **WATERLOO** The first production EMUs based on these prototypes began to enter service on the Southern Region in January 1980. A total of 43 of the new four-car units, designated as Class 508, was delivered from York Works as the first step in replacing the by then elderly 4 SUB units on suburban services from Waterloo. The new regime was very apparent on Sunday 27 July, when Platforms 1, 2 and 3 at Waterloo were all occupied by new Class 508 units.

CHESSINGTON SOUTH In 1930 the Southern Railway obtained powers to build a loop line from Motspur Park to Leatherhead via Tolworth and Chessington, although construction did not start until 1936. The line was opened between Motspur Park and Tolworth in 1938 and was extended to what was then regarded as a temporary terminus at Chessington South, which opened on 28 May 1939. The station here was only partially completed, with all passenger trains terminating in the down platform. The unused and rather unkempt up platform can be seen on the left of this view; note the distinctive 'Chisarc' concrete canopy, a feature of all the platforms on this branch. Beyond Chessington South a length of embankment was prepared ready for the line onwards to Leatherhead, but the establishment of the Green Belt around London after the Second World War prevented the previously anticipated housing development from taking place, so the line has remained a branch terminating at Chessington South.

New Class 508 unit No 508009 has terminated and waits to form a service back to Waterloo on Tuesday 25 March 1980.

The interior view, taken at the same location, shows the spacious accommodation, with low-backed seating generally arranged in a 3+2 pattern across the width of the carriage. This at least provided more seats per unit than the 2+2 pattern of the experimental sets, although still significantly less than the six-a-side closed compartments featured in many of the 4 SUB units that these trains replaced – the 508s were greeted with mixed feelings by quite a few regular customers.

1980 Arrivals & Departures

Births

Rebekah Teasdale	Model	2 January
Jenson Button	Formula 1 driver	20 January
Steve Tully	Footballer	10 February
Andy Scott-Lee	Musician	29 March
Ben Freeman	Actor	8 April
Michelle McManus	Musician	8 May
Steven Gerrard	Footballer	30 May
Martin Devaney	Footballer	1 June
Oliver James	Actor	1 June
Philip Oliver	Actor	4 June
Jessica Taylor	Musician	23 June
Katherine Jenkins	Musician	29 June
Ben Wishaw	Actor	14 October
Alan Smith	Footballer	28 October
Adele Silva	Actress	19 November
Steve Lovell	Footballer	6 December
John Terry	Footballer	7 December
Ashley Cole	Footballer	20 December
Laura Sadler	Actress (d2003)	25 December

Deaths

Barbara Pym	Novelist	(b1913)	11 January
Sir Cecil Beaton	Photographer	(b1904)	18 January
Graham Sutherland	Artist	(b1903)	17 February
Dixie Dean	Footballer	(b1907)	1 March
Alfred Hitchcock	Film director	(b1899)	29 April
Hugh Griffith	Actor	(b1912)	14 May
Ian Curtis	Musician	(b1956)	18 May
Billy Butlin	Businessman	(b1899)	12 June
John Laurie	Actor	(b1897)	23 June
C. P. Snow	Novelist/physicist	(b1905)	1 July
Peter Sellers	Actor	(b1925)	24 July
Kenneth Tynan	Theatre critic	(b1927)	26 July
Yootha Joyce	Actress	(b1927)	24 August
Hattie Jacques	Actress	(b1922)	6 October
Johnny Owen	Boxer	(b1956)	4 November
Rachel Roberts	Actress	(b1927)	26 November
Sir Oswald Mosley	Politician	(b1896)	3 December
John Lennon	Musician	(b1940)	8 December

HAMPTON COURT If the customers had mixed feelings about the Class 508 units, some of the Southern Region's engineers soon also considered that the new trains were not especially suitable for the services on which they were being used. In particular they were incompatible with any other stock on the Region, and in due course the decision was taken that they would be transferred to Liverpool to work with the virtually identical three-car Class 507 units in service around that city. This transfer began in April 1982 and was completed in December 1984; only three carriages from each four-car unit were transferred, the remaining trailer carriages being incorporated into some of the replacement Class 455 units. Unit No 508013 was still one of the newest trains on the Southern Region when photographed at Hampton Court forming the 1444 service to Waterloo on Wednesday 2 April.

Kent coalfield memories

SNOWDOWN COLLIERY Located beside the main railway line between Canterbury East and Dover, work started on the sinking of Snowdown Colliery in 1907, the first coal being brought to the surface in 1912. Snowdown was the deepest pit in the Kent coalfield and was known among the mining community as 'Dante's Inferno' because conditions below ground were so hot and humid. Initially many of the miners travelled from Dover to work at the colliery, which led to the construction of Snowdown & Nonington Halt, primarily for their use, in 1914. During the 1920s a mining village was built nearby at Aylesham; this also was to gain its own station, which opened in 1928. Extensive sidings linked the colliery with the main line near Snowdown & Nonington Halt, and Ray Ruffell visited on Wednesday 6 February 1980.

Class 11 diesel shunter No 12131, seen in the top photograph, had been built by BR Darlington Works in 1952 and worked in East Anglia and on Eastern Region lines around London until withdrawn in 1969 and sold to the National Coal Board. It was subsequently purchased from the NCB for preservation in 1982, and at the time of writing can be seen on the North Norfolk Railway.

It can also be seen furthest from the camera in the lower photograph; in the centre is a Fowler shunter, also built in 1952, while closest to the camera NCB locomotive No 8 was new in 1958.

SNOWDOWN COLLIERY Supplied new to Snowdown Colliery in 1927, 0-6-0 saddle tank *St Dunstan* was the last survivor of three similar locomotives at this location. Escaping the scrap torch after withdrawal, *St Dunstan* is currently located at the nearby East Kent Railway, awaiting full restoration. The East Kent Railway, easily reached by train at Shepherd's Well (next station on from Snowdown), is well worth a visit, especially by fans of Southern electric multiple units; delights include carriages from COR, CEP and EPB units. *St Thomas*, erstwhile stablemate of *St Dunstan* at Snowdown, can be seen on static display at the Dover Transport Museum.

In the second photograph we see diesel shunter No 15224, which was built at BR Ashford Works in 1949 as part of a batch originally ordered by the Southern Railway but delivered into service after nationalisation. This locomotive worked on the Southern Region of British Railways and was sold to the National Coal Board after withdrawal. Ray Ruffell himself stands in the cab doorway as coal trucks are shunted at Snowdown on Wednesday 6 February 1980. Preserved after withdrawal by the NCB in 1985, No 15224 went initially to the Lavender Line and at the time of writing can be seen at the Spa Valley Railway at Royal Tunbridge Wells.

Snowdown Colliery was closed in 1987, and the last of the Kent collieries, at Betteshanger, followed two years later in 1989. Snowdown & Nonington Halt (now known as Snowdown station) and Aylesham station both remain in use in the 21st century.

Seen at Salisbury

Right: **SALISBURY** The spacious station at Salisbury was rebuilt in 1902 to a design by J. W. Jacomb-Hood, and has handled all rail passenger traffic in the city since the adjacent Great Western terminus station was closed in September 1932. On Wednesday 23 July 1980 Class 33 diesel-electric locomotive No 33010, in service with BR from June 1960 until April 1988, carries headcode 89 while standing at Platform 4 with the 1215 Portsmouth Harbour to Bristol service. At the bay Platform 5 on the right, one of the push-pull-fitted Class 33s, No

33104, stands with a 4TC unit; the additional 'plumbing' on the front of this locomotive will be noticed when compared with the much plainer front of No 33010 on the left.

Left: **QUIDHAMPTON** English China Clay had a chalk pit and factory at Quidhampton, just west of Salisbury. Between 1972 and 2009 it was served by sidings, illustrated here on Wednesday 23 July 1980; driver Jim Moody is just visible looking through the cab window of No 33104, while second man Mike Dawkins leans out of the door window behind him; the guard is Martin Cannings. The last train from the sidings at Quidhampton to Eastleigh ran at 1012 on Monday 30 March 2009.

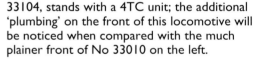

Catch it while you can: 'The Dalesman'

CARNFORTH During the late 1970s and early 1980s Honiton Round Table organised a number of ambitious railtours. One of these was 'The Dalesman' on Saturday 22 March 1980, which started from Yeovil at 0553 and ran a total of more than 900 miles, visiting Crewe, Carnforth, Hellifield and the Settle & Carlisle line before eventually arriving back at Yeovil and stations to Exeter in the early hours of the following morning. A stop of just under an hour was made at Carnforth in the early afternoon. The first station here was opened in 1846, and was rebuilt in 1880 and again in 1937. The location is famous as the setting for the 1945 film *Brief Encounter* (in which it was called Milford Junction); with the snow on 22 March 1980 a brief encounter was probably more than enough – but not before a glimpse at the signal box, a delightful essay in Gothic architecture. In recent years there has been restoration work at Carnforth station, which since 2003 has been home to a visitor centre, while the refreshment room has been restored to its 1940s appearance as seen in the film, which also brought Rachmaninov's Second Piano Concerto to a wide audience. *Brian Jackson*

CARNFORTH Probably the most iconic steam locomotive in the British Isles, No 4472 *Flying Scotsman*, was photographed after a snowstorm at Steamtown, Carnforth, on the same day. Built for the LNER at Doncaster Works in 1923, *Flying Scotsman* was preserved by Alan Pegler after withdrawal by British Railways in 1963. A very expensive item to maintain, the locomotive has been part of the National Railway Museum collection since 2004. *Brian Jackson*

East from London

Below: **SHOEBURYNESS** A total of 112 four-car Class 302 units were provided for the electrified services from Fenchurch Street to Shoeburyness; as built, each four-car unit had accommodation for 344 2nd Class and 19 1st Class passengers. The units started to be used on off-peak services on the line from November 1961, and the full electric timetable was introduced from 18 June 1962. Unit No 265 is seen at Shoeburyness forming the 1540 service to Fenchurch Street on Tuesday 15 April; the carriage closest to the camera is a Driving Trailer 2nd, with seats for 108 passengers in nine non-corridor compartments each seating six a side.

Above: **FENCHURCH STREET** Unique among the London terminal stations in not having a direct link to the Underground, although Tower Hill station is only a short walk away, Fenchurch Street station was rebuilt in 1853-54 to a design by George Berkeley of the London, Tilbury & Southend Railway. When Ray Ruffell took this photograph looking towards the buffer-stops on Tuesday 15 April 1980, there had been relatively few changes to the station beyond the provision of the infrastructure for electric trains; three examples of Class 302 units built for services from Fenchurch Street to Shoeburyness await their next departures. Today, more than 30 years later, the scene is much changed; an office development was built over the inner ends of the platforms during the early 1980s, while another and much larger development using the air space over the eastern end of the station was completed in 1991. Income from these developments enabled this busy station to be extensively refurbished, and the main entrance frontage is probably the only part of the premises that is unchanged from when this photograph was taken.

SHOEBURYNESS An area at Pig's Bay to the east of Shoeburyness had been acquired for use as an artillery range in 1849 and was later developed by the military for weapons testing. The area included its own private railway network, linked by a line to one of the sidings in the depot at Shoeburyness. This link includes an unmanned level crossing over Shoeburyness High Street, where Army diesel shunter No 234 is seen crossing the road under the protection of a flagman on Tuesday 15 April 1980. Another use for the old Army lines at Pig's Bay has been the storage of withdrawn British Rail and London Transport rolling stock prior to scrapping.

TV favourites

To Serve Them All My Days
Based on the book by R. F. Delderfield, the serial about an idealist who had been shattered by the First World War and had subsequently taken a job in a private school won a BAFTA award for the BBC.

Love in a Cold Climate
Also set in the 1920s, this was based on Nancy Mitford's books about life in her family at that time.

Shelley
Hywel Bennett starred in the title role of this enjoyable comedy series about the life of a university drop-out.

Strangeways
A eight-part fly-on-the wall documentary series filmed in the eponymous Victorian prison made for grim viewing, but illustrated the sordid reality of prison life.

Public School
TV cameras also filmed a documentary series at Radley College near Oxford, where living conditions were somewhat more agreeable.

Yes, Minister
Reputed to be Prime Minister Margaret Thatcher's favourite programme, this comedy series about the relationship between politicians and civil servants was very popular with viewers.

Training Dogs the Woodhouse Way
Something of a surprise hit, a programme about training dogs attracted large viewing figures and made a celebrity of the elderly presenter Barbara Woodhouse. 'Walkies!' said in a particular tone of voice, briefly became a catchphrase.

DISS An unusual feature of this market town in the Waveney Valley is that the settlement has grown up around a large lake some 6 acres in size and up to 18 feet deep, which is known as the Mere. Mentioned in the Domesday Book, the town has many historic buildings and is an interesting mix of Tudor and Victorian architecture; there has been a market here for more than 500 years, and the population in 2012 was just under 7,000. The 1652 train to Liverpool Street on Thursday 7 August 1980 is headed by Class 47 diesel-electric locomotive No 47160; new in 1964 and numbered D1752 until 1973, this locomotive was subsequently renumbered 47605 in February 1984 and withdrawn from service in December 2003.

BRESSINGHAM Many people travel via Diss station to visit Bressingham, where the gardens of almost 20 acres and the preserved railway stock of varying gauges combine to make a great day out. One of the lines at Bressingham offering rides on Thursday 7 August was the 15-inch-gauge Waveney Valley Railway; 4-6-2 locomotive No 1662 *Rosenkavalier* was built by Krupp in 1937 and had previously been used in Dusseldorf.

extensive factory area also includes 10 miles of railway tracks, and motive power on these privately owned lines in 1980 included some Class 03 shunters that had been withdrawn after relatively short lives with British Rail. Two such locomotives are seen here. That on the left was built at BR Doncaster Works in 1959, withdrawn from British Rail service in 1972 and purchased by Ford, in whose fleet it was numbered 4 when this photograph was taken on Monday 30 June. This locomotive was preserved after eventual withdrawal by Ford; it arrived at the North Norfolk Railway in 2000, where at the time of writing it is stored out of use.

Ford's private lines connected with the main British Rail network, and in the second photograph an unidentified locomotive from the Ford fleet crosses the electrified London, Tilbury & Southend line on the same day; note the train of brand-new Ford cars in the siding beside the line.

DAGENHAM Henry Ford's son, Edsel, cut the first turf for the construction of the company's plant at Dagenham on 17 May 1929. The factory took more than two years to complete, and it was in October 1931 that the first Dagenham-built vehicle – a Model AA truck – came off the production line. The site was on low-lying marshy ground that required extensive piling to support the new buildings, but the location by the River Thames provided a deep-water port facility. The

POPLAR DOCKS Some rail freight traffic was still handled at Poplar Docks in 1980. From the 1960s onwards all such trains had used the former North London Railway route via Old Ford and Victoria Park. For some years grain was transported by this route from Poplar Docks to Welwyn Garden City, where it was used in the manufacture of Shredded Wheat. Most of the Poplar freight workings were hauled by Class 31 diesel-electric locomotives, but Class 03 shunters were used in the docks area, and on Monday 30 June shunting is in the hands of No 03154. Built at British Railways Swindon Works and entering traffic on 1 July 1960 as No D2154, this was one of a class total of 230 locomotives built

between 1957 and 1962 for light shunting duties. Many were withdrawn by British Rail after quite short working lives (see also page 33), but No 03154 was to remain in service until 11 September 1983.

The last rail freight movement at Poplar Docks took place on 30 August 1981 and the track between Victoria Park and Poplar Docks was lifted in 1984; from 1987 onwards that part of the former North London Railway formation between the present stations at All Saints and Bow Church has been reused as part of the Docklands Light Railway.

Tyne & Wear developments

NEWCASTLE-UPON-TYNE Third-rail electric trains had started running between Newcastle and Tynemouth as early as 1904, and electrification was extended to include the South Tyneside lines to South Shields in 1938. By the early 1960s these services were losing money, and as a result they were de-electrified, diesel multiple units taking over the South Tyneside route in 1963 and those to Tynemouth in 1967. The resulting deceleration of services did nothing to encourage passenger growth. However, the Tyne Wear Plan of 1971 saw the potential of an electrified local railway system as part of an integrated transport network, especially if a station could be provided that was more conveniently sited for the main retail and commercial centre of Newcastle than the existing main-line station.

The Tyneside Metropolitan Railway Act received Royal Assent in 1973 and work on the new system commenced in August 1974. British Rail's Tynemouth loop and the South Tyneside route to South Shields were to be incorporated into the new Metro network, and an important advantage would be the construction of new underground sections of route in Newcastle and in Gateshead, together with a new bridge across the River Tyne. The Metro would be electrified at 1,500V DC, with overhead current collection.

Ray Ruffell visited the project while work was in progress on Tuesday 22 January 1980. He photographed the line emerging from the twin-bore tunnels under Newcastle and also the new bridge across the River Tyne, which has a span of more than 164 metres and is built 24 metres above water level to give an unrestricted passage to shipping. The first section of the Tyne & Wear Metro, between Haymarket and Tynemouth, was opened on Monday 11 August 1980. The new bridge, together with the South Tyneside route as far as Heworth, opened in November 1981, with the new service reaching South Shields in March 1984.

NEWCASTLE-UPON-TYNE The Tyne & Wear Metro was a pioneering installation of light rail operation in the UK, despite such systems having been relatively common in mainland Europe for many years. Accordingly, an extensive test track was set up at Newcastle, including level crossings, gradients and curves together with a small car shed/workshop to accommodate the two prototype passenger cars that were delivered from Metro-Cammell in 1975. These cars were numbered 4001 and 4002; the main picture is a head-on view of car No 4002 standing in the small shed, while the interior of car No 4001 is seen while running on the test track – both photographs were taken on Tuesday 22 January 1980.

A further 88 cars of the same type were delivered to give the Metro a fleet total of 90; the two prototypes were given minor modifications to completely conform to the production build and were fully integrated into the fleet. The seating, arranged in facing pairs, can be seen in the interior view, which also illustrates the two car body sections connected by an articulated vestibule; each car is mounted on three bogies.

Its role having been completed, the test track was closed in July 1980, and is now the site of the Stephenson Railway Museum, which opened in 1986. The 90 Metro cars were still in service in 2012, with an ongoing refurbishment programme likely to see them remaining in use until around 2025, while the 21st century has seen the Tyne & Wear Metro further extended to serve Sunderland and South Hylton.

1980 Happenings (2)

GATESHEAD The massive Dunston Staithes were commissioned by the North Eastern Railway as part of the Dunston Extension Railway to export coal from collieries in Tyneside and County Durham. The staithes, 1,709 feet long and 50 feet wide, came into use in 1893, and are reputed to be the largest timber structure in Northern Europe. They could accommodate up to six collier ships at a time, and during the 1920s an average of 140,000 tons of coal per week was shipped from here. When photographed by Ray Ruffell on Monday 14 January 1980, Dunston's were the last working staithes on the River Tyne; closure came during that year, but the structure was repaired in the late 1980s and used as part of the National Garden Festival in 1990. The staithes still stand, but are on the English Heritage 'At Risk Register' after suffering damage from fires in 2003 and 2010. There is recognition of the importance of the staithes in illustrating the major part that coal once played in the prosperity of the area, and efforts are being made to secure their restoration.

July
- Government announces introduction of Enterprise Zones in an effort to relieve unemployment in some of the more depressed areas of Britain.
- Alexandra Palace in London is severely damaged by fire.

August
- Great Britain and Northern Ireland win five gold, seven silver and nine bronze medals at the Moscow Olympic Games.

September
- Ford launches the Mark 3 Escort.

October
- Council tenants in England and Wales of at least three years' standing gain right to purchase homes at a discount.
- Express coach services are deregulated.
- British Leyland launches Austin Metro.
- Gloagtrotter (GT Coaches) starts coach service between Scotland and London marketed as 'The Stage Coach'; this was the beginning of today's Stagecoach transport business.
- MG production at Abingdon ends after 56 years.

November
- Michael Foot is elected leader of Labour Party.

December
- Former Beatle John Lennon is shot dead in New York; six days later thousands of fans hold 10-minute vigil in Liverpool in his memory.

SOUTH SHIELDS During the 19th century the Harton Coal Company opened a number of pits around South Shields on South Tyneside. From the late 1870s a system of private railway lines was established to take coal to exchange sidings with the main railway network and to take coal and colliery waste (the latter for dumping at sea) to staithes on the River Tyne at South Shields. Much of this colliery system was steam-operated for many years, but between 1908 and 1910 the lines between Westoe Lane (near Westoe Colliery) and the River Tyne were electrified, using overhead wires at 550V DC.

The collieries became part of the National Coal Board with effect from 1 January 1947, so these lines became state-owned a year before the advent of British Railways. Two of the locomotives used on the line are seen in these photographs taken on Tuesday 12 February 1980. No 2, on the left, was built by Siemens in 1908 and can be compared with the system's newest electric locomotive, No 15, which was built by English Electric in 1959.

Left: **WESTOE COLLIERY** In the early 1950s the National Coal Board built a new coal washing plant at Westoe that could handle the entire output from the collieries in the area together with some coal from elsewhere. It came in via the exchange sidings, from where the 21-ton hopper wagons were hauled to Westoe by two new electric locomotives, Nos 11 and 12, that had been built by English Electric in 1951 for this purpose. Locomotive No 12 is seen at Westoe Colliery on Tuesday 12 February.

Right: **SOUTH SHIELDS** Like locomotive No 15, seen opposite, No 14 was also built by English Electric in 1959; detail differences in design can be seen when this locomotive is compared with 1951-built No 12 in the photograph above. The unusual practice of mounting the pantograph on the 'bonnet' rather than the cab roof was to allow the locomotives to work through a tunnel with restricted height to reach Harton Low Staithes.

This interesting railway system was closed in 1989; it was partly replaced by a conveyor system, but Westoe Colliery, the last operational pit in South Tyneside, was closed in May 1993.

A Southern selection

WATERLOO Tuesday 2 September saw the naming of two of the Southern Region's fleet of Class 33 diesel-electric locomotives. Closest to the camera, No 33027 has been given the name *Earl Mountbatten of Burma*, in remembrance of Lord Louis Mountbatten who had been assassinated a year earlier, on 27 August 1979, while on holiday in Mullaghmore, County Sligo. Locomotive No 33027 had entered service in March 1961 as No D6545, and remained in the British Rail fleet until July 1991.

The other locomotive is No 33056, new in October 1961 as No D6574 and subsequently withdrawn in February 1991. This locomotive was named *The Burma Star* to honour those who took part in the Burma campaign between December 1941 and September 1945. The 1944 Battle of Kohima in North East India is recognised as a turning point in this campaign; the memorial to those of the 2nd British Division lost in the Battle is inscribed 'When you go home, tell them of us and say, For your tomorrow, we gave our today' – words ascribed to John Maxwell Edmonds (1875-1958) and known today as the Kohima Epitaph. The naming ceremony is taking place with due respect on the platform beside the locomotives.

UPWEY In 1966-67 19 of the Southern Region's fleet of Class 33 locomotives were converted to be suitable for use in push-pull operation with multiple unit stock, principally the unpowered TC units on the section of line between Bournemouth and Weymouth. The locomotives so converted were readily recognisable by the additional 'plumbing' on their front ends, and were given the classification 33/1 in the TOPS scheme. Here an unidentified Class 33/1 locomotive powers a 4TC unit past the remains of Upwey Wishing Well Halt (closed in 1957) and into Bincombe South Tunnel, near the top of the stiff climb out of Weymouth, during April 1980. *Brian Jackson*

HAVANT Although the push-pull-fitted Class 33 locomotives were especially associated with the line between Bournemouth and Weymouth, the usefulness of the class members, with their multifunctional controls enabling then to propel or haul electric stock over non-electrified lines, led to them being used extensively in other areas, including journeys between Waterloo and Salisbury/Yeovil and between Reading and Portsmouth – all with TC stock. They also came into their own when weekend engineering work required services to be diverted. On this occasion trains between Waterloo and Weymouth were being diverted via Liphook, Havant and Fareham; the 4REP unit could power the train as far as Havant, but in 1980 the line between Farlington Junction and St Denys had not been electrified, so Class 33/1 locomotives were being used to haul or propel trains between Havant and Southampton Central and vice versa. On the left of the photograph No 33109 is about to propel a REP/TC formation from Havant to Southampton via Fareham;

new as No D6525 in October 1960, this locomotive remained in service until 2001 and was subsequently preserved on the East Lancashire Railway carrying the name *Captain Bill Smith RNR*. *Brian Jackson*

SOUTHAMPTON CENTRAL Similar engineering diversions were taking place in December 1980 when this photograph was taken showing Nos 33113, 33107 and 33108 awaiting their next turns of duty in the up west siding at Southampton Central. Of this trio, No 33108 has survived into preservation and now resides at Barrow Hill with the name *Vampire*. Entering the photograph from the right is diesel-electric multiple unit (DEMU) No 1402 on a Portsmouth to Bristol service; this was one of a batch of four such units (Nos 1401-1404) that had been augmented from two to three carriages in 1979 by the addition of a former 2EPB driving trailer (which had been used in that capacity in a Reading-Redhill-Tonbridge DEMU since 1964) as an intermediate trailer coach. *Brian Jackson*

Below: **DEEPDENE** Since early 1965 services on the Reading-Redhill-Tonbridge line had been provided for more than 14 years by the makeshift (but reliable) 'Tadpole' diesel-electric multiple units. By 1980 the service had been rerouted to also run between Reading and Gatwick Airport, and Western Region diesel-mechanical multiple units provided most journeys, as exemplified by this photograph of a three-car set arriving at Deepdene forming the 1555 Reading to Gatwick service on Friday 19 September. This station is within easy walking distance of Dorking station on the Horsham line, and when the Second World War broke out the Southern Railway moved some of its headquarters departments to nearby Deepdene House (now demolished).

Right: **NORTH CAMP** The Farnborough Air Display always attracts crowds, and additional train services operate to take people to and from this popular event. On Tuesday 2 September 1980 the 1744 return special to Manchester was hauled by Class 47 diesel-electric locomotive No 47089 *Amazon*. Having entered service with British Rail in April 1965 as No D1675, *Amazon* was subsequently withdrawn in June 1987. On the other platform the diesel-mechanical multiple unit operating the 1655 Reading-Redhill service again illustrates the rolling stock used for local services along this line in 1980.

No 1 records of 1980

January

| Another Brick In The Wall | Pink Floyd |
| Brass In Pocket | Pretenders |

February

| Too Much Too Young | Specials |
| Coward of the County | Kenny Rogers |

March

Atomic	Blondie
Together We Are Beautiful	Fern Kinney
Going Underground/Dreams Of Children	Jam

April

Working My Way Back To You/Forgive Me Girl	
	Detroit Spinners
Call Me	Blondie

May

Geno	Dexy's Midnight Runners
What's Another Year	Johnny Logan
Suicide is Painless	MASH

June

| Crying | Don McLean |

July

Xanadu	Olivia Newton John
	& Electric Light Orchestra
Use It Up And Wear It Out	Odyssey

August

| The Winner Takes It All | Abba |
| Ashes to Ashes | David Bowie |

September

Start	Jam
Feels Like I'm In Love	Kelly Marie
Don't Stand So Close To Me	Police

October

| Woman In Love | Barbra Streisand |

November

| The Tide Is High | Blondie |
| Super Trouper | Abba |

December

(Just Like) Starting Over	John Lennon
There's No One Quite Like Grandma	
	St Winifred's School Choir

GATWICK AIRPORT 4CIG unit No 7359 was leading the 12-car 1110 London Victoria to Newhaven boat train when photographed at Gatwick Airport on Thursday 24 July. On the right a three-car diesel-mechanical multiple unit waits to form the 1207 service from Gatwick Airport to Reading. A very important rail/air interchange point, the station at this site has been known as Gatwick Airport since 1958, having opened as Gatwick Racecourse in 1891. On 30 September 1935 a station here opened as Tinsley Green (renamed Gatwick Airport nine months later), providing rail connections for the airport; this earlier structure was located to the south of the present station illustrated here.

Right: **STROOD** Class 33 diesel-electric locomotive No 33046 is seen shunting in the sidings at Strood. This locomotive had entered traffic in July 1961 as No D6564 and remained in service until March 2007; preserved after withdrawal as No 33046 *Merlin*, it is currently at the Midland Railway Centre, Butterley. Standing to the right is 0-4-0 diesel-mechanical shunter *Telemon*, built in 1955 and owned by W. M. Cory Ltd. In 1987 *Telemon* was also preserved, and at the time of writing is in the care of the Cambrian Railways Society. *Brian Jackson*

Left: **STROOD** The importance of this location as a transport centre dates back to 1824 when a canal linking the Thames and Medway, thus avoiding the 41-mile detour around the Isle of Grain, was opened between Gravesend and Strood, including two tunnels between Higham and Strood. In 1845 authorisation was given to construct a single-line railway along the canal towpath and along a staging erected in the tunnels. The following year the canal was acquired by the South Eastern Railway, and double track was laid throughout to Strood, completed in July 1849. Thus the railway continues to use the tunnels that were originally provided for the Thames & Medway Canal. At Strood in 1980 the canal basin and lock gates still survived, albeit disused; the entrance to Strood Tunnel can be seen in the background, while No 33046 shunts in the goods yard. *Brian Jackson*

Below: **QUEENBOROUGH** The 8-mile branch line from Sittingbourne to Sheerness-on-Sea was opened in 1860, and was electrified in 1959 as part of Phase 1 of the Kent Coast Electrification project. Situated on the Isle of Sheppey, 6 miles from Sittingbourne, Queenborough is the penultimate station on the branch; this view looking towards Sheerness-on-Sea was taken on Wednesday 14 May 1980. Surprisingly the substantial main station buildings are on the down (Sheerness-bound) platform here, with just a small shelter provided for passengers travelling to Sittingbourne (or London). A BR Standard 2HAP unit approaches, forming a service to Sittingbourne; the inverted black triangle indicates that the brake van is at the end of the train nearest to the camera.

Above: **WIMBLEDON PARK** In winter the third-rail electrified lines of the Southern Region are vulnerable to ice forming on the conductor rails, resulting in arcing that can cause serious damage to trains, including burnt-out shoe gear. To minimise this problem, special de-icing trains, converted from elderly electric multiple units, operate during severe weather. Some additional de-icing units were converted from withdrawn 4SUB driving motor carriages at the end of the 1970s, and Nos 008 and 009 were newly converted when photographed at Wimbledon Park on Monday 18 February 1980. The carriages had been extensively rebuilt during the conversion process, the appearance of the cab ends in particular being considerably altered. Nearest to the camera the carriage numbered ADB975597 had first entered service as part of 4SUB unit No 4124 in 1946.

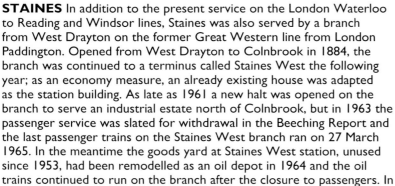

STAINES In addition to the present service on the London Waterloo to Reading and Windsor lines, Staines was also served by a branch from West Drayton on the former Great Western line from London Paddington. Opened from West Drayton to Colnbrook in 1884, the branch was continued to a terminus called Staines West the following year; as an economy measure, an already existing house was adapted as the station building. As late as 1961 a new halt was opened on the branch to serve an industrial estate north of Colnbrook, but in 1963 the passenger service was slated for withdrawal in the Beeching Report and the last passenger trains on the Staines West branch ran on 27 March 1965. In the meantime the goods yard at Staines West station, unused since 1953, had been remodelled as an oil depot in 1964 and the oil trains continued to run on the branch after the closure to passengers. In

1980 work was proceeding on a short new link between the Southern Region's Staines to Windsor line and Staines West to allow the oil trains to run via the Southern Region route.

These photographs show the new link under construction on Tuesday 22 July and Friday 19 September 1980. Note the oil tank wagons visible in the Staines West depot in the background of the July photograph – the line to West Drayton runs beside the hoardings and off to the right of the photograph. The new link from the Southern Region to the oil depot was brought into use in January 1981, when the branch from West Drayton was closed to all traffic south of Poyle. The new track was in use for just over ten years until the Staines West oil depot closed in June 1991.

WALTON-ON-THAMES

By 1980 haulage of trains between London Waterloo and Exeter was in the hands of the Class 50 diesel-electric locomotives, as exemplified here by No 50029 *Renown* speeding westwards at Walton-on-Thames on Monday 3 March with the 1300 service from Waterloo. The train consists of a mixture of BR Standard Mark 2 and Mark 1 carriages, which was quite usual for the route at that time. Entering service in June 1968 as No D429, No

50029 had been given the name *Renown* in October 1978 and remained in service with British Rail until March 1992. It was preserved after withdrawal and at the time of writing, together with sister locomotive No 50030 *Repulse*, is being restored at Peak Rail in Derbyshire by the Renown Repulse Restoration Group.

WATERLOO

And so we end our tour of parts of the railway system as they were in 1980 at the approach to London Waterloo station, photographed on Wednesday 18 June. A 4TC unit heads the 1635 service from London to Weymouth, while a Class 508 unit forming the 1636 to Chessington South can be seen in the background. In contrast, passengers travelling to London on the 1605 service from Chessington have been provided with a 4SUB unit dating from the late 1940s, which is still in overall blue livery.

Acknowledgements

I hope you have enjoyed this look back at the interesting and varied transport scene that was part of our everyday lives during that year.
It would not have been possible to produce this book without making use of two very extensive photographic collections. Many of the illustrations started in the camera of the late Ray Ruffell. Ray was a railwayman by profession, but his interest in transport went far beyond his day-to-day work. In his off-duty time he travelled widely, and in so doing created an extensive photographic record of the railway system during a period when great change was under way. Other photographs in this volume were taken by Brian Jackson, a fellow transport historian who has also travelled extensively across the UK armed with his camera to record the ever-changing transport scene. My warm thanks to Brian for allowing me to use some of the photographs he took during 1980.

Many scenes that were everyday and commonplace when Ray or Brian photographed them have now been swept away for ever, and the memories captured on film, precious at the time, are now beyond price. It is pleasing to record that the late Ray Ruffell's collection of photographs has been kept complete and is now in the safe keeping of The NOSTALGIA *Collection*, forming an important part of the company's photographic archives.

I would like to say a sincere thank you to the team at The NOSTALGIA *Collection* for inviting me to write this book. The cheerful and willing help I have received from Peter Townsend, Will Adams and David Walshaw has been very much appreciated, and I feel deeply honoured to work with such kind people.

Index

FOXFIELD RAILWAY Our final photograph shows Ray Ruffell (second from left) with his daughter Margaret and wife Joan during a visit to the Foxfield Railway, near Stoke-on-Trent, on Saturday 29 March 1980. The locomotive in the background is *Helen*, built by the Motor Rail & Tramcar Company, Bedford, in 1923 for the Cornforth Limestone Company, County Durham. Originally powered by a petrol engine, this was replaced by a diesel unit when this four-wheel locomotive was rebuilt in 1934. *Helen* was sold to Dunlop at Coventry in 1949 and passed into preservation at the Foxfield Railway in 1968.